This Journal Belongs to:

Robin Elaine Cross
November 4th, 2000

Heather Ann Reagan

JOURNAL FOR A WOMAN'S HEART
published by Multnomah Publishers, Inc.

© 2000 by Multnomah Publishers, Inc.
International Standard Book Number: 1-57673-702-0

Image of lace by Artbeats
Image of flowers by KPT Power Photos

Multnomah is a trademark of Multnomah Publishers, Inc.,
and is registered in the U.S. Patent and Trademark Office.
The colophon is a trademark of Multnomah Publishers, Inc.

Every effort has been made to provide proper and accurate source attribution for
selections in this volume. Should any attribution be found to be incorrect, the publisher
welcomes written documentation supporting correction for subsequent printings. For
material not in the public domain, grateful acknowledgment is given to the publishers
and individuals who have granted permission for use of their material.

Quote by Nancy Spiegelberg. Used by permission of the author. www.godthoughts.com.

Quote by Philip Yancey. Used by permission of the author
and Multnomah Publishers, Inc., Sisters, OR. 97759

"Faith Is…" by Pamela Reeve. Excerpted from *Faith Is…* by Pamela Reeve © 1994 Multnomah
Publishers, Inc., Sisters, OR 97759. Used by permission of the publisher.

Quotes by C.R. Gibson Company excerpted from *Words I Have Lived By* by Norman Vincent Peale
© 1990. Used by permission of C.R. Gibson Company, 39 Knight Street, Norwalk, CT 06856

Quotes by Heartland Samplers excerpted from *Bless Your Heart series 1* flip calendar. © 1987. Used
by permission of Heartland Samplers, Inc., 3255 Springs St. N.E., Minneapolis, MN 55413

Unless otherwise indicated, all Scripture references are from
The Holy Bible, New International Version © 1973, 1978, 1984 by the
International Bible Society. Used by Permission of Zondervan Publishing House.
All rights reserved.

Printed in China

For information:
MULTNOMAH PUBLISHERS, INC.
POST OFFICE BOX 1720
SISTERS, OREGON 97759

00 01 02 03 04 05 06 — 10 9 8 7 6 5 4 3 2 1 0

Journal for a Woman's Heart

BASED ON ALICE GRAY'S BESTSELLING SERIES
STORIES FOR THE HEART

Multnomah® Publishers *Sisters, Oregon*

A smile of encouragement at the right moment
may act like sunlight on a closed-up flower;
it may be the turning point for a struggling life.

Kind words are the music of the world.

They have power that seems to be beyond natural causes,

as if they were some angel's song that had lost its way and come on earth.

—FREDERICK WILLIAM FABER

*Lighthouses don't ring bells and fire guns to
call attention to their light...they just shine!*

You will find as you look back upon your life, that the moments when you have really lived are the moments when you have done things in the spirit of love.

—HENRY DRUMMOND

*In times of affliction we commonly meet with
the sweetest experiences of the love of God.*

—JOHN BUNYAN

And now these three remain: faith, hope and love.
But the greatest of these is love.

—1 CORINTHIANS 13:13

God pardons like a mother, who kisses the offense into everlasting forgiveness.

—HENRY WARD BEECHER

I long to put the experience of fifty years into your young lives, to give you at once the key of that treasure chamber every gem of which has cost me tears and struggles and prayer; but you must work for these inward treasures yourselves.

—HARRIET BEECHER STOWE

Love one another deeply, from the heart.

— 1 PETER 1:22

Trust people as if they were what they ought to be
and you help them become what they are capable of being.

—GOETHE

The human soul is a silent harp in God's choir, whose strings need only to be swept by the divine breath to chime in with the harmonies of creation.

—HENRY DAVID THOREAU

The art of being happy lies in the power of
extracting happiness from common things.

—HENRY WARD BEECHER

Have courage for the great sorrows of life and patience for the small ones;
and when you have laboriously accomplished your daily task, go to sleep in peace.
God is awake.

—VICTOR HUGO

Some of God's attributes are too wonderful to understand.
But even if they remain darkness to the intellect,
let them be sunshine for your soul.

*The greatest thing in the world is not so much where we
stand as in what direction we're moving.*

—OLIVER WENDELL HOLMES

O God of Second Chances and New Beginnings,
Here I am again.

—NANCY SPIEGELBERG

He drew a circle that shut me out—Heretic, rebel, a thing to flout.
But Love and I had the wit to win; We drew a circle that took him in!

—EDWIN MARKHAM

In dreams and love there are no impossibilities.

—JANOS ARANY

Above all else, guard your heart, for it is the wellspring of life.

—PROVERBS 4:23

We are shaped and fashioned by what we love.

—GOETHE

I believe in the sun even when it is not shining.

I believe in love even when I feel it not.

I believe in God even when He is silent.

—WRITTEN ON A WALL IN A CONCENTRATION CAMP

Where your pleasure is, there is your treasure.
Where your treasure is, there is your heart.
Where your heart is, there is your happiness.

—SAINT AUGUSTINE

The human heart yearns for the beautiful in all ranks of life.

—HARRIET BEECHER STOWE

How far you go in life depends on your being tender with the young, compassionate with the aged, sympathetic with the striving, and tolerant of the weak and the strong—because someday you will have been all of these.

—GEORGE WASHINGTON CARVER

Blessed is the man who has the gift of making friends; for it is one of God's best gifts. It involves many things, but above all the power of going out of one's own self and seeing and appreciating whatever is noble and loving in another man.

—THOMAS HUGHES

When one door closes, another opens.
But we often look so regretfully upon the closed door
That we don't see the one that has opened for us.

—ALEXANDER GRAHAM BELL

I am full-fed and yet I hunger. What means this deeper hunger in my heart?

—ALFRED NOYES. C.R. GIBSON COMPANY

Few delights can equal the mere presence of one whom we trust utterly.

—GEORGE MACDONALD

When I pray, coincidences happen.
When I stop praying, coincidences stop.

—WILLIAM TEMPLE, ARCHBISHOP OF CANTERBURY

If all our misfortunes were laid in one common heap,
most people would be contented to take their own and depart.

—HEARTLAND SAMPLERS

For he will command his angels concerning you,
to guard you in all your ways.

PSALM 91:11

Because God has made us for Himself,
our hearts are restless until they rest in Him.

—SAINT AUGUSTINE

What sunshine is to flowers, smiles are to humanity.
They are but trifles to be sure, but scattered along life's pathway,
the good they do is inconceivable.

—JOSEPH ADDISON

Let my heart be broken with the things that break the heart of God.

—ROBERT W. PIERCE

Love comforteth like sunshine after rain.

—WILLIAM SHAKESPEARE

Every morning lean your arms awhile upon the window sill of heaven
And gaze upon the Lord.
Then, with the vision in your heart
Turn strong to meet your day.

In times like these, it helps to recall that there have always been times like these.

—PAUL HARVEY, C.R. GIBSON COMPANY

*Our friends see the best in us, and by
that very fact call forth the best from us.*

—HUGH BLACK

When we feel as if God is nowhere, He is watching over us with an eternal consciousness, above and beyond our every hope and fear.

—GEORGE MACDONALD

After two weeks of reading the entire Bible,
I came away with the strong sense that God does not
care so much about being analyzed. Mainly, he wants to be loved.

—PHILIP YANCEY

If I can stop one heart from breaking, I shall not live in vain.
If I can ease one life the aching, or cool one pain,
Or help one fainting robin into his nest again, I shall not live in vain.

—EMILY ELIZABETH DICKINSON

Come to me, all you who are weary and burdened, and I will give you rest.

—MATTHEW 11:28

We are like angels with just one wing.
We fly only by embracing each other.

Faith is...

Remembering I am God's priceless treasure when I feel utterly worthless.

—PAMELA REEVE, FROM "FAITH IS"

If a man does not keep pace with his companions,

perhaps it is because he hears a different drummer.

Let him step to the music which he hears, however measured or far away.

—HENRY DAVID THOREAU

Henceforth there will be such a oneness between us—
That when one weeps the other will taste salt.

God gave us memories so
that we might have roses in December.

It is when we forget ourselves
that we do things that will be remembered.

Faith is the bird that feels
the light and sings
while the dawn is yet dark.

—TAGORE

A friend will strengthen you with her prayers,
bless you with her love, and encourage you with her heart.

Fear not tomorrow for God is already there.

If you have much, give of your wealth;
If you have little, give of your heart.

Happiness resides not in possessions and not in gold;
The feeling of happiness dwells in the soul.

—DEMOCRITUS

A faithful friend is a sturdy shelter.
He that has found one
Has found a treasure.

—THE APOCRYPHA

Hope is brightest
When it dawns from fears.

—SIR WALTER SCOTT

I breathed a song into the air, It fell to earth I know not where...
And the song from beginning to end, I found again in the heart of a friend.

—HENRY WADSWORTH LONGFELLOW

If instead of a gem, or even a flower, we should cast the gift of
a loving thought into the heart of a friend—that would be giving as the angels give.

—GEORGE MACDONALD

Touched by a loving heart, Wakened by kindness,
Chords that were broken, Will vibrate once more.

—FANNY CROSBY

*The heart is its own memory, like the mind, and in it are
enshrined precious keepsakes, into which is wrought the giver's loving touch.*

—HENRY WADSWORTH LONGFELLOW

It takes two to speak truth—one to speak, and another to listen.

—HENRY DAVID THOREAU

"Oh, how delightful it would be to live in a house where everybody understood, and loved, and thought about everybody else!" *She did not know that she was wishing for nothing more and something a little less than the kingdom of heaven.*

—GEORGE MACDONALD

If we fill our hours with regrets of yesterday and worries of tomorrow,
we have no today in which to be thankful.

—HEARTLAND SAMPLERS

If I had a single flower for every time I think about you,
I could walk forever in my garden.

—CLAUDIA GRANDI, HEARTLAND SAMPLERS

If I were to be described in one word, what would it be?

—HEARTLAND SAMPLERS

Fragrance always clings to the hand that gives you roses.

—CHINESE PROVERB, HEARTLAND SAMPLERS

Happiness comes of the capacity to feel deeply,
to enjoy simply, to think freely, to risk life and to be needed.

—STORM JAMISON

It is right to be contented with what we have, never with what we are.

—MACKINTOSH

Take time to laugh. It is the music of the soul.

—ANONYMOUS

Friendship that flows from the heart cannot be frozen by adversity,
as the water that flows from the spring cannot congeal in winter.

—JAMES FENIMORE COOPER

The smallest seed of faith is better than the largest fruit of happiness.

—HENRY DAVID THOREAU

Laughter is the best medicine for a long and happy life. He who laughs—lasts.

—WILFRED PETERSON

Life is short and we never have enough time for gladdening the hearts of those who travel the way with us. Oh, be swift to love. Make haste to be kind.

—HENRI FREDERIC AMIEL

Delight yourself in the Lord and he will give you the desires of your heart.

—PSALM 37:4

Forgiveness is the fragrance the violet sheds on the heel that has crushed it.

—MARK TWAIN

Lord of my heart's elation, Spirit of things unseen,
Be thou my aspiration, Consuming and serene!

—HENRY WADSWORTH LONGFELLOW

One can never consent to creep when one feels an impulse to soar.

—HELEN KELLER, C. R. GIBSON COMPANY

He who cannot forgive breaks the bridge over which he himself must pass.

—GEORGE HERBERT

The real voyage of discovery consists not in
seeking new landscapes but in having new eyes.

—MARCEL PROUST